Unashamed Spirit,

Untamed Heart

Poetry
By Tracy Brown

Unashamed Spirit, Untamed Heart

ISBN: 978-0-359-73472-6

Printed in the United States of America.

First printing, 2019.

Phyl Campbell, Publisher
www.phylcampbell.com

Dedication

I would like to dedicate this work to my husband. You are the light of my life, my inspiration, the joy in my heart. You loved me into loving myself and for that, I am forever grateful. Your love allows me to love you even more than I ever dreamed possible. Thank you. To my sweet, delightful children whom I have carried in my heart from the time I knew were in my body. What a sweet, sweet delight. Always present, never forgotten. To Phyl, my phenomenal publisher for sticking with me, always being there for me and encouraging me. To all that have been a support in this journey, I thank you from the bottom of my heart.

Poems

Thought Provoking

Rivers Run Deep

Rivers run deep
Deep through my soul
Flowing endlessly
Through my whole
Being
Rivers run deep
Gushing, rushing, moving
And waves bellowing
With memories
With remembering
Memories of life
Of laughter
Of love
With remembering
Of safe-keeping
Of pleasures
Of joys
Rivers run deep

Rivers run deep
Moving me
Carrying me
Through this life
Can't recognize the beginning
Can't see the end
Rivers run deep
Deep through my soul
Flowing endlessly
Through my whole
Being
Rivers
Run
Deep

In the Present

In the Present
This place
This space
Where nothing existed before
No opened, no closed doors

The Present
In it
Lies everything
And yet nothing at all

The Present
Everything you are able to accomplish here
In this moment
This now space
This place
Where you come
When you reside
In your own being
Forever seeing your place
In this space

The Present
Welcome to Being
I am
In likeness of the One

In the Present

The Child

The child. The child in you, the child in me. I hear them both saying, come on, I AM IN HERE... PLEASE LET ME BE!"

The child...the child in you, the child in me. I hear them both saying... "COME ON, I AM IN HERE, I EXIST!!! STILL!!!!
PLEEEEASE!!! LET ME BEEEEEEEEEEE!
THE CHILD..."

FULL of emotions, though not able to comprehend the definition...
FEEEEEEEEEEEELS...

THE CHILD...
FEELSSSSS
FEELSSSSS within our heart as it beats softly, calmly,
to beating violent, chest pounding vibrations!!!!
and all other beats... in be tweeeen...

The child...
The child in you, the child in me... I hear them both saying... "Come on, I am in here... PLEASE LET ME BE!!!"
The child....
Born natural, to this land
The child...
Should have been free by any as well as his own hand
The child...
Has his own innocent desires, wants, needs and ways of being
The child...
In the evolution of the being, the child never leaves, but is the essence of the evolved, being...
The child
The child in you, the child in me...

I hear them both saying, "come onnnnn!!! Acknowledge, affirm me to you, of you, in you and....
Let me
Be!"

My Hair Spoke to Me Today

My hair spoke to me today...
After my yoga and slight meditation
It said to me,
"Why do you not take better care of me?
Why do you love other parts of you more than me?
Look at me
Can't you see I need love?
You will care for your eyebrows and nails,
Choose good makeup for your face,
Buy nice clothes and shoes...
May workout too!!
But what about Me?
I barely see the light of day.
When will you want ME to look MY best?"

My hair spoke to me today...
After my yoga and slight meditation
It said to me,
"Why do you not take better care of me in my
Natural,
Divinely given,
Pure state?"

My hair spoke to me today...
After my yoga and slight meditation
My hair looked at me through the mirror and said,
"I was created to be soooo much more than you allow me...
So pleaseeeeeeeeeeee
Love me
Care for me
And
SET ME FREE!!!!!!!"

My hair spoke to me
TODAY.

Truth vs Reality

Sometimes I feel like you must

    keep truth separate from reality.

Truth is at the core of your very being.

Reality is the construct

    in which we were born and live

    or can be defined that way.

The false sense of living is in a way

    that is in line with this world.

Or we could say reality is

    we are truth in flesh

    which sometimes leaves us

    Alone.

The Denial

What could cause a person
to start out in the blue
Come into the light
only to fall into darkness?
Is it fate?
Destiny?
Prophesy?
Scripture?
Is the act of deliverance
from darkness
the testimony
in
truth?
The final curve
to complete
the circle of one?
Of oneness
with
the
Divine?

Diagnosis

They say when you do this it means you are that.
When you have too much energy, you are hyper
Not enough energy, sleep too much, you are depressed
Get excited too easily or don't react in a timely manner
Must mean that...

Don't have any energy or need for sex?
Want too much? Got to have it all the time?
All are cause for a
Diagnosis

To get you on a pill or in a hospital bed
Be careful or you will be led
Into a mirage of doctors with prescription pads or hospital beds
For no other reason than the physician's family to be fed

How about standing straight up?
Having full confidence in yourself and saying...
If I'm sleeping, it's because I need my rest
If I'm not, it's because I already got it
Or if I look at you and don't respond

It's because I see you as crazy and
Not worthy of my time or comment
Or I could decide that I feel like sounding off on you
It's because I just flat out wanted to
Or I may just want to hear my own voice
In a different way at that time in that moment
It's my choice you know

As for sex, it depends on how good the product is
It may be good enough to fill me up
For a day, a week, a month or two
Or maybe I'm just in an insatiable mood
To fuck, and fuck and fuck
Getting some good ass down to the bone
Shaking and baking good ass love making.
In any case, it's me, all of me, in the flesh
Not caught up in your mess
Of what should and should not be
It's me
And I am my own
Diagnosis

Drama

The name is drama
How many times
How many ways
Does drama come to us these days
Drama
Is there ever a new scenario?
Or do the originals keep reoccurring
Recycling themselves from household to household
Place to place
Face to face
Drama
Yes an adrenaline rush may come with it
Or a heart attack due to the stress from it that made you sick
Drama
Leave it for the stage

Never take in or take on the rage that it seeks to claim
Drama
Release it
Love
Meditate
Exercise
Find those who can relate to the love you feel for yourself
It is a positive fate
Be whole
Complete yourself
Then you can find your way
Out of
Drama
And into
True
Fulfilling
Relationship

That soothes your mind
And nourishes your soul

The Twist

With a twist, I am removed from today
With a twist, I turn the mundane to play
With a twist, I go where others dare not
With a twist, I turn from whole, to a dot
Wind in my hair, sun from behind
In a flash, I turn from reality
To something in your mind
That is
And now was
Because
With a twist
Of my wrist
I am gone

(Motorcycle ride...boom!)

You Want Me

You want me
Yes, you do
You want me
Through and through
You need me
Though I not you
You seek me out
To do your do
An unholy temple
Is what you wish upon me

From what is God's
From what simply purely is
You want me
Yes you do
You want me
Through and through
You need me
Though I not you
You seek me out
To do your do

To build using my hands
My mind
My abilities
My gifts
The ones that God gave me
The creation of His
You want to exploit
To extract from
To collect a harvest

You want me
Yes
You
Do
But
I
Belong
To
My
Father...

To my God:
Thank you
For creating the path
For showing me the way
To grow
To live
Every
Single
Day

Knowing

You never know
until you know
and when you know
then you know
and when you really know
you can come to understand
come to know
what knowing really is

Life

Life

Is it passing you by or are you by-passing life?

Time

24 hours in each day

What will be done in this next 24 hour cycle?

Joy

Moments of happiness, of content, of fulfillment

Pain

Moments of being wounded at varied depths

Life

Is it passing you by or are you by-passing life?

The Stained-Glass Mirror

The Stained-Glass Mirror
Its beauty we behold
Whenever we are near her
We gaze at her, seeking to witness her mysteries unfold
Designs embedded within her glass
Much time was taken
To build this illustrious creation
Upon which the memory of, would ever last
Such a wonderous, loving toil
Built with such tenacity time could never spoil
There is beauty in the stained-glass mirror
Its title holds a purposeful truth

Silence

There is so much power in
Silence...
Seek to be
Strong

Protocols

There are protocols
In dealing with and interacting with other individuals
The best ones out of all the choices, rules
Regulations and authoritarians out there
The best protocols
For human interaction
Are rooted in Spiritual groundedness...
So, it is always best to go there first.

The Vision

When people look at you and see you
What they are really seeking out is
Your state of mind

Some Days

Some days come and go and
I do not have a recollection of its contents
But I know that it was here
And so was I

Dance to the Drum

Beat Beat Beat

Hear the sound of the drum
Pulling me, calling me forward

Hum drum drum,
"Out of your seat!" Says the drum
"Come meet!" Says the drum
"Your future into your past, It is waiting for you
"Get up! Get up! At last! Now!"
Says the drum
"Do not delay!" Says the drum
"Your heart is connected to me
"Come and see! Let's play!

"Play! Play! Play!

"Sing! Dance! Move! To my beat! My rhythm!
"That through you flows regal healing...
Get out of your seat!

"These words I will repeat!
"Dance to the drum!

"I need you as much as you need me
"And together we WILL as we always CAN be
"As
ONE
So
COME
and
DANCE
to the
DRUM"

The Day I Stopped Worrying About the Unknown

The day, today
Is the day
What day you say?
The day ISWATU
What? I ask, if I may?
The day I Stopped Worrying About the Unknown
The day ISWATU...
But how can...what if...what about...!!!
Nope!!! No and noooo.
Too many other things already in tow
Already dealing with, already have to take care of
Plate full, will not allow the overflow with the
Tone of
the
Unknown

When I'm Gone

Yesterday we catered a Celebration of Life
A room filled with women,
Men and children all coming dressed very nice
Bringing all sorts of homemade treats
Finger snacks and desserts
Catered with all the trimmings by us
Tables dressed in skirts
Celebrating the life of one that has made their transition
That has passed on from this life to another
It got me thinking...

Who will come, who will know about me
When I'm gone?
When this life is over and I enter into the next
What will be said about me?
What will be the text?

So inside myself I go
For it is so comfortable for me there
Inside to see
What gifts, if any, I bear
What is on the inside of me
And of it all?
The different doors and rooms in there
What and who do I allow others to see?

Am I, do I offer anything to this world for the earth?
Of me, has anything, will anything come from, be
remembered of my birth?

When I look in the mirror, what do I see?
What resides there?
What if anything, do I exude, do I give, do I allow to
show through?

When I'm gone
When this life for me ceases to exist
Have I lost more than I have gained?
Will I be forgotten in a flicker of a wrist?
How important is one love, life born?
What is its purpose?
In and through so many of life's moments
So many of life's storms
When I am gone
Did I share, did I care, did I heal
Parts of myself, my past, immediate and ancestral,
My present?
Did I do any self work
to make my future in this life and the next any better?
When I am gone, what will be said about me being here
When I am gone.

Pain

Scissors

I am looking for my scissors
In the closet and dresser drawers
Upstairs, downstairs,
Where could they be

I need to get them,
I need to use them,
I need to be set free

Maybe I should go up a level,
Look in the garage
Find a good pair of gardening shears
Anything strong enough to do this job

My heart aches me so,
I need to be free of it,
I need to let it go

To cut my heart out
Seems to be the only way
I can truly be free of the pain
I feel so so very deep these days

I am looking for my scissors
Oh please help me find
A way to end this pain
A way to ease my mind

You Used to Be My Everything

You used to be my everything
You used to could do no wrong
My blinded truth to you gave me strength
Kept me strong
Brought me through many trials
Both big and small
Helped me, when I fell to get up
To try and stand tall
You used to be my everything
Anything for you I would survive
Sometimes I had to run
Sometimes I had to hide
Hoping, praying
That one day our love would come to be
Two into one
You and me
You used to be my everything

A promise denied for too long
I finally switched my purpose
And began to sing a new song
You used to be my everything
Now I know this much to be true
Before I couldn't love me
I only wanted to love you
You used to be my everything
And now the train I must ride
Is the train of love for me
In which the Holy Spirit resides
My true rock, my true resting place
And sanctuary of peace
You used to be my everything
Now I know
My everything resides within me

You Can't Be A King

You can't be a King
You can't hold a crown
Your license has been revoked

You carry too much hate
Too much anger
You carry the wrong sound
Of a
King
Something you will never be
Something you will never ever claim
Because on your hands
Lie too many tears
Too much bloodshed
Hands
Fully
Stained...

You
You could never be a king
You could never hold the crown
You don't have the skills
Always turning a smile
Into a frown

Weak
That's what you are
A
Bitch
Standing tall
Chest poked out
Fist balled up
Lips stuck out

You

With your fake ass pride
Which is really
Low self-esteem

Can't take care of your household
Can't love and cherish your mate
Your woman

Your children
Could never see a beautiful
Peaceful
Love-filled life unfold

You
You will grow lonely
And
Old
Because too much hate
Too much evil
Lives inside of you

Ride or die
You bitch ass fooooooooooooooooooooooool

You...
Could
Never
Be
King...

You
Simply
Do not qualify...

So...

BYE

Invisible me

Where am I
I do not see me
I know that I am here
I know that I Be
But, where am I
Invisible me
For I do not see me
I see women
Angry, violated, disrespected and being disrespectful
I see hard hearted, non-supportive
Loud and aggressive
Lost, raped
Hidden, used
Ah, yes
That's right, that's true
I do belong
I see
Invisible me

Time

Time is a fucked up concept
Time is a fucked up idea
That shit keeps you traveling
Along a plane that's bullshit clear

In time it will be better
With time everything will be alright
Just give it time and things will turn around
Time heals all wounds
Fuck time

Damage

So much damage
So much change
So much hurt
Caused by damage
So much pain
Damage
What the f___k is wrong with you
To cause, be responsible for
Be the initiator of
To take on and
Follow thru with
So
much
Damage

The Shift

There comes a time in the journey of suffering

A crossroad

A tilt point

Pivotal if you will

Where there is a shift from enduring

To surviving

Suffering

Into making a plan

Seeking the way to end

Suffering

Methods of survival

Tactics to end

Suffering

Vary

From time to time

Place to place

Person to person

How many lie in the wake

Of the shift

Love

Come to Me in My Dreams

Come to me in my dreams

Let me see you, let me look at you

Come to me in my dreams

Let me feel you: Your strength, your gentleness

Hold me in your arms, keep me safe, hold me close

Let me know where I am in you

Taste me, touch me

Feel me breathe in and out

The rhythm calmed by your being

Are you here? Are you in my dreams?

Are you the glue that binds me together at the seams?

When everything wants to come pouring out...

When I feel lost

Hope waning, light dim...

Come to me in my dreams and assure me that everything is alright

Come to me in my dreams

Let me see you, let me look into your eyes and know...

I may have you

Come to me

If nowhere else

In my dreams

Let Love Flow

Everything you need
Everything you want
Comes from the inside of you
It's in the inner of your being
Everything you love
Is on the inside of you
Love is not a destination
Love is not an address
Love is not connected with a physical being
Love is a spirit
That spirit lives inside of you
It's on the inside
Always has been
Always will be
So...
Today...
Let
Love
Flow

Once

I once loved a man
Took a chance, opened my heart
To the rhythm of the dance
Danced days and nights on end
Music intertwined from beginning to end
The happiness in my heart was so real, felt so true
It would grab me and keep me, it would carry me through
Love
A feeling like no other
So very different when you love your man, a man, than that of a
sister or a brother
Can take you to the highest heights and protect you from the lowest
lows
Can keep you as life continually changes and unfolds

I once loved a man
Took a chance, opened my heart
Hoped and prayed that we could be together always
Through thick and thin, never would we part
I once loved a man
Not just any man
Not just male by design
A man, a REAL man
I once loved a man
His imperfections haunted me as deeply as his perfections
Oh what to do...

I once loved a man
A real man, a good man, a great man: a King
And then I decided to

Never. Ever. Let. Him. Go...

I once loved a man
And I still honestly, earnestly, whole heartedly, passionately,
exotically, erotically still do
Love that man

Love Song

Love, so patient and kind
Love
So sweet to my mind
Love
Believes all things
Love
The reason I sing
Love
For you I am so grateful
So thankful
Love
For holding me up and never letting me fall
Love
For you I am so grateful
So thankful
Love
For holding my hand
and helping me to stand
Times have been tough
Hard nights so long
There have been days when
I couldn't find a song
But love touched my heart through and through
Kept me safe, kept me around until
I could feel, again, you
Love
Now I know I can overcome
I can withstand
Cause
Love
So patient and kind
Love
So sweet to my mind
Love
Believes all things
Love
The reason I sing

Unbreakable

Unbreakable
I see the definition in the dictionary as
    "unable to disassemble
To not fall apart, to not come loose"
To stand steadfast in truth
Holding onto the Rainbow
Never letting go
Never giving up
In it for the win
    the double you (W)
Unbreakable
Torn, battered, withered, bruised
Journeys long, hard
    seemingly unyielding
The Light is worth existing, maintaining
In this field, see
The world will strive to hold you, take you,
    turn you away from
Keep you away from what's divinely written as Yours
But as a ram in the bush, lying wait
You know the true, real, pure, unalterable score
And remain
Unbreakable
Untakeable
Unmistakable in your quest
Til the light breaks through
Makes it able to shine
Brightly
Brilliantly
Delightfully
Excitedly
    on Thee
Who always remains
Relentlessly, incessantly, obsessedly, possessedly
Unbreakable
A true example of God's infinite love
Unbreakable

Love

Love

The ups

Love

The downs

Love: the good

Love: the bad

Love: the highs

Love: the lows

Love: Continual

Love: Never absent

Love

Unceasing, unending

Always available

Infinitely enduring

Love

Yours and mine

The If Only Song

If only I could see the sunrise in your eyes
If only I could watch the joy from your heart
When it springs forth as in surprise
If only, if only, if only I could
If only I could have the chance to feel your breath in my ear as your
voice cascades sweet honey dipped words to me
"Love" it says, you say
As the words vibrate through me
If only, if only, if only I could hear
Those sounds come into my body in varied levels of depths, tones,
hues
I am inevitably, immediately soothed through you, through your
sound, through your touch, through your being
If only, if only, if only I could
If only I could smell the scent of your existence
Nostrils filled with the fragrance of your being
The proof of your physical proximity
All without ever seeing
If only, if only, if only I could
Do all of these things
Feel all these things
See all these things
Touch all these things
If only, if only, if only I could, experience these things all night long
There would be no reason for this song

Granddad

I never felt like a grown-up with Granddad
He always greeted me with a smile so bright
And eyes so sincere it would melt me into infancy
I never felt like a grown-up with Granddad
For every ounce of big, tall, dark, handsome and
    immensely strong to the world he was
He was ever more soft, caring, fun,
    gentle and kind with me
I never felt like a grown-up with Granddad
Til I had an adult question, a concern or strife
Then, I could go to or pick up the phone
    and call Granddad
And kindly, gently, thoughtfully and sweetly he would
School me about life
He would listen to me and talk to me
His voice alone would soothe me
As his words would bring me to a place of
    understanding
To a space of peace
And once he had me aware
Once he had shown me the way back
Guided me on a chariot to there
I would become Granddads baby girl again
    and again and again and again
I never felt like a grown-up with Granddad
Born in the 1910s
His life trials in the deep south as a powerfully built,
    black as night with skin smooth as velvet male
I never knew and he never talked about, never
    expressed, never shared
All I knew was
I never felt like a Grown-up with my Granddad
Because that's just how much he cared.

My God Dream

God Put a Dream in My Heart
He put it there at the very point
I so desperately needed it the very very most

God put a dream in my heart
And He said "hush now about it, don't boast"

God put a dream in my heart
When I needed it the very very most
Something for me to lean on,
to hold on to, to cling to, and to rest in
During the roughest,
most hurtful, most difficult times of this life
When the world of me would try to roast
Try to burn me to the core
When life would try to destroy me,
discredit me,
try to steal the life
right out of me
try to kill me...

God put a dream in my heart
To remember that for me
He had commissioned more...
More love, more joy, even more kindness, more
More sweetness and extra loving care

God put a dream in my heart
And said, "Just hold on to it baby,
"'til you make it there."

God put a dream in my heart
and God's Word ALWAYS comes true...

God put a dream in my heart
and that dream, sweet dear, is
YOU.

Lost and Found

Lost
Deeply
Down through the depths of my soul
Lost
Though time exists this experience never grows old
Lost
Unable, incapable of feeling any other way
Lost
I surrender more and more to this feeling everyday
Lost
This feeling that makes me so weak. I am left unarmed
Lost
All the layers of hurt and pain
Peeled back, ripped open

Lost
For I never dreamed, never imagined, never even
began hoping that I would be
Lost...
That's were my soul dwells
When I look into your eyes...
Helplessly, openly, unashamedly, thankfully,
gratefully, lovingly, singly, unequivocally
Lost
In your eyes
My dear, sweet dear
I am lost
and
Found

Ready

God, I am ready for the husband you choose for me
God, I am ready for the husband you choose for me
God, I am ready, you saw to it that I would be
Humble, generous and kind
Full of caring and sweetness for me and what's mine
You were gracious enough to give me some left over for others too
So they could experience your sunshine flowing through me from
you
God I am ready for the husband you choose for me
He has been through an awful lot, I can see
Yet many things are still left unknown

So please God, place us together in a place we can call home
I am ready God, for the husband you choose for me
So please God
Today let it be his face that I see.

Come to Me

Come to me in the morning my sweet
Let us meet and greet the sunrise...together
Sit with me, talk with me
For in our exchange I will verbally be silent
However, life-giving will be reciprocal
Take of me
For I am yours to have
Given freely
From the earth of this land
As you take
We will both appreciate
What it is to be loved and shared
Provided for with the utmost care
For through design, the more you take
The more I give
And so that we both shall live
We come together as one

To simply be
You and me
The herb tree and
This body

Make Love to Me

Make love to me
For all the times you thought of me and couldn't
Make love to me
For all the days you could have but couldn't
Make love to me
For all the nights you wanted me
Make love to me
For all the days that didn't come to be
Make love to me
For all the highs and lows
Make love to me
Like you forever want to keep me close
Make love to me
Time and time again
Make love to me
Like you belong in

Were made for
My skin
Make love to me
Til the universe opens deep and wide
Make love to me
In places I could never hide
Make love to me
Let your love overflow
Make love to me
Because you love me ohhhh just so
Make love to me
Because you know I've wanted you
Desperately too

Make love to me
Til time becomes anew
Make love to me
Make me your rebirth
Make love to me
For in your love deeply, sweetly abides
Make love to me

As the wind flows, As the sun rises
Make love to me
For all the times you were so near, yet so far
Make love to me
For the sun, for the moon, for the stars
Make love to me
For the path that lights our way
Make love to me
In thanksgiving for the night, In honor of the day
Make love to me, make love to me,
make love to me, make love to me
In a sphere, flowing all through the universe
Make love to me
Til eternity
Make love to me, love to me, inside me, beside me

Cause your love is me, guides me, sets me free
So, my love, brought to me
Angelically, from the heavens above
My dearest, sweet dove
Make
Love
To
Me

Our Warriors

What is this with our warriors?
Our biggest, our strongest
Put on display
To be broken and beat down
For someone's entertainment?
What is this with our warriors?
Bruised and broken
In pain, yet continually striving
No whole opportunity to rest, restore, to heal
When is there adequate time to love and be loved?
To care and be cared for?
Our warriors...
So much brain power
Grows ever forth hour by hour
So Strong
To be honored

Yet displayed
Come home
Find a way to it
To rest, to restoration, to healing, to love, to family
To peace...
We honor you
As Is
Rest my warrior
You are loved

You

You are the breath
My breath
In I breathe you
Out I breathe the world
In I take of your essence
Out I breathe what does not make sense
You make sense
You are my world
You were given to me
To hold
To love
To allow to be
The Perfect Package
Created deliberately, diligently
To me, for me
To be
Mine
I am oh so fine
With
You

Inspirational

Spirit Being

I am a Spirit Being
I am a Spirit Being
Having, Living a Human Existence
I feel, I cry, I bleed
I yearn for, I desire
I am a Spirit Being
Having, Living a Human Existence
What is this world that I have come into for healing, regeneration,
and restoration?
I have needs and wants
Hurts and anguish
The depths of my soul have been sought after, hunted
Will I rise again?
Will I learn new lessons
Conquer old ones?
Will I this time, heal my soul?
I am a Spirit Being
Having, Living a Human Existence

Angels in Sacred Spaces

There are angels in sacred spaces
Traveling around to different places
Spreading joy, bringing peace
In those sacred places
Where others may not seek

There are angels in sacred spaces
Traveling around to different places
Looking over
Looking after
Those who seem lost
To bring them hope
To fill them with laughter

There are angels in sacred spaces
Traveling around to different places
Thank you, God for your angels
Thank you for the gift, the thought
To bring wings of love
To those whom others deem lost

There are angels in sacred spaces

Days

Gratitude

Love

Experience

Kindness

Joy

Peace

Roads Traveled

Wounds

Lessons Revealed

Roads Traveled Again

Lessons Learned

Wounds Healed

Moving On

What You

What you see
You will see
What you view
You will behold
What you feel
You will experience
What you know
You will sow
What you see
You will see
And what you see
Will see you

Higher

As we look up into the sky
We see wonderous things
Beautiful, strong, lush, green tops of trees
Beyond them is a skyline of blue clouds
Bellowing across the sky
Higher
On the ground at the dirt of the earth is where we reside
Where we are housed in this now
As we seek to rise
Higher
With each step we take forward there is
An accompanying step we can choose to take up on this journey
Higher
Navigation is the key
Things once blind to we now see
As we make our way
Higher
Things that used to bother us
No longer do as we make our way
Higher
Relationships fall off or improve
Both doors bring positive reviews

As we make our way
Higher
With time passing our perspective changes
Brainwaves are re-routed
more and more toward the light of
Higher
As we look up into the sky
We see wonderous things
Beautiful, strong, lush green tops of trees
Beyond them is a skyline of
Blue skies and white clouds
Bellowing across the sky
Reminding us that what once was, is now below us
Underneath us is no longer, is no more
Because
We have finally, simply decided to reach for it
To strive for, to move on into and climb
Higher
and
Higher is and feels
Good

Shine Baby Shine

In the morning when I wake
It's dark, can't wait to see daybreak
Shine baby shine

When my eyes open
I am blessed to see another day
I thank God who goes by many names
For all the blessings coming my way
Shine baby shine

I wait in expectancy for that sun, my sun, never failing, always true
To come up
Rising
Shining through and through
Shine baby shine

Up Up Up
Steady and slow
Constant
That's my sun, getting us ready for the next day, the next show
Shine baby shine

The birds feel it before we can see it
And sing praises to God for the sun
Which represents a new day begun
Shine baby shine

From darkness it comes
Turning to red then orange
Brightening up the sky, announcing the day
I thank you God for all the blessings coming my way
Shine baby shine

A clean, white sphere in its fullness
Bringing warmth, light, health and healing
Into this world in which we are currently dealing
Shine baby shine

Thank you, God for the sun
So powerful, lovely and true
Thank you for the love
May we all keep it in our hearts like two lovely doves
Shine baby shine

I look forward to all of your blessings today
The sun tells me they are coming my way
So thankful, so grateful to you God for the sun
Shine baby shine

So in the spirit of love, joy, peace, forgiveness,
Thankfulness, gratefulness, gentleness, kindness
I look forward to THIS day
Thank you for giving me mine
Shine oh baby shine.

Happy Space

I love my happy space
It's a place I go to
   when I am in need of a smile
It's a place I go to
   when I am in need of some joy
My happy space
I can access it anytime, anywhere
Whenever I want to go there
My happy space
It's on the inside of me
I can get there
   while sitting on the ground
   or smiling at a tree
   or sitting in a chair
   as chaos flows all around me
My happy space
It's truly a beautiful place

Opening

I can feel my heart opening
I can feel my spirit rising
For so long my heart has been closed
For so long no one was to impose
Love
Wonderful, beautiful, sweet
Kind, caring, giving
All things I could, should, would give freely to others
Enjoying those moments fully
    on the faces of my sisters and brothers
But for me
I made sure it was not to be
Made sure because a seed, early,
    deeply had been planted in me
A seed of shame, guilt and secrecy
Made me ashamed for many years to receive love
Yes me
The one who always had a smile to give
A kind word to share
But for myself not one to spare
But life is moving differently for me know
Better
I am doing, by grace my healing work
I am getting lots of help with it
Each person I am sure has been divinely chosen
To help me on this journey, on this quest
And yes
Through this process I have,
    after many hard years of living or existing
Struggling, suffering,
    almost drowning in my own tears
I can finally feel my heart opening
Thank you, God, for your patience, loving kindness,
    grace and mercy into
Opening

Every Day I Am

To search for a defining moment in life
is egotistic. To feel as if I must become
this or that, then searching for and
seeking the this or that, ...ego.
Instead, try ...

Every day, I am.
Every day, I am.
Every day I am
Here
On this journey called
life
Every day
Every day I am
Who I am
Enough
Whole
For
Today
So let's enjoy this day

The day that has been given
So many beautiful things in this day
Become lovingly one with your spirit
And allow the blessings of today to just flow
And overwhelmingly,
They will.
Always remember

Today
I
Am

The Coolness of the Rain

The Coolness of the Rain
Rain Falling
Rain coming down
From Heaven
To Nourish my Body
To Heal my Soul

The Coolness of the Rain
Its Sound Filled with the Same
For my Ears
Rhythmic
Like Dancing to a Sweet Tune
I Close My Eyes and Listen
Whether Morning, Midnight, or Noon
When rain comes it's never too soon

The Rain
It Soothes Me
Washes Me
Cleanses My Spirit
Renews My Soul

Rain
Pure
On a Continuous Effort to Help Me Grow
To Make Me Feel Whole
In the Coolness of the Rain

The Water

Sounds of Waves bellowing
Calling out their location
The Water
Ripples coming toward me
Seeking me out
Seducing me
Wanting, needing my attention
Requesting my presence
Calling me home
The Water
A place of serenity
A sacred nest of love
Of reflection, of peace
Of healing
Visit often
If only in your mind
Close your eyes
Rest your mind
And be
Near or in: the Water

Digging My Feet Into The Sand

When I dig my feet into the sand
They sink down a little
I feel the grains of sand
making their way between my toes
When I dig my feet into the sand
I find a resting place
A solitude
In the midst of all the grains of sand
Thousands of them
all their own size and shape and color
All their own individual entity
Yet synonymously empirically continued as a unit
Too many too dry
and they have the potential to rub my skin dry
Peel it away even
Too many too wet
and my feet will sink deeper and deeper
into the depths of the abyss
Yet I still enjoy digging my feet into the sand
Digging my feet into the sand
It is a metaphor for life
Making a choice to stay in
To be in this life
To step solidly into the familiar
Which is also the unknown
To simply purely whole heartedly
Stand
Breathe
Receive
Establish and create what is real
What is true
What is never ending
What is timeless
Is what I do when
Digging my feet into the sand

This poem was inspired while reading
What Happened to Nina Simone?

Giving Life

Life
What is it?
A breath, a heartbeat
Blood flowing through the body
Blue to purple to red
Life
Is it free or does it cost
Some have said
That to be in this life
Is to take on strife
Does it consume you
Does it take you down
For into the depths
Taking on all that you can handle
All that you can bear
Life
How do you continue on

How do you live
In order for life to maintain itself
Someone, something has to give, has to open
Open wide
Something has to split, to divide
In order to create, in order to give what we call
Life
Heart beating, blood pumping existence

What to do with it now
What is it to be used for
What is there to gain

For through it all, in it all and for it all
If love is not purely
Earnestly, sincerely, wholly what you seek
What you strive for, what you yearn for
What you desire...
Well then my sweet

Giving life is not what you can claim
Nor is it what you will own
Only an empty shell will be your domain

To haunt you again and again
The truth to giving life
Resided in your open heart
Through
Love
That's L-O-V-E

For only through it shall you see the true meaning of this existence
Whether for a second, a minute, an hour or a hundred thousand
years
With no fear in the way
You are the only one who hears
The call of
Love...
Which is the essence of
Giving Life

Tracy Brown

The enigmatic poet pursues talents both on the stage and on the ropes of the aerial stage. Out of the limelight, Tracy is the warmest soul, volunteer, advocate, and support system for many in the Athens area. She is also a Reiki practitioner and Yoga instructor. She earned a bachelor's degree in Biology from Kentucky State University and a master's in Exercise Science from the University of Rhode Island.

Poems included in *Unashamed Spirit, Untamed Heart* have been compiled from several years of self-discovery and healing. Brown finds her truth in myriad experiences and does what she can to shine past hurt, past heartbreak, and past shame. She hopes her poetry will inspire others to release pain they've been holding on to, grab hope in their hands, and fly.

Made in the USA
Columbia, SC
23 September 2020